**Date Due**

APR 1'78

MANILLA GALLEONS

RUSSIANS 1780'S

# A HISTORICAL MAP OF
# CALIFORNIA
## Legend

| | | | |
|---|---|---|---|
| PORTOLÁ - 1769 | | TRAILS OF THE | |
| ANZA - 1774 | | FORTY-NINERS | |
| SMITH - 1826-28 | | ✝ MISSIONS | |

WHALING 1791

PACIFIC OCEAN

THE GREAT SEAL OF THE STATE OF CALIFORNIA

EUREKA

STEAMSHIPS 1849

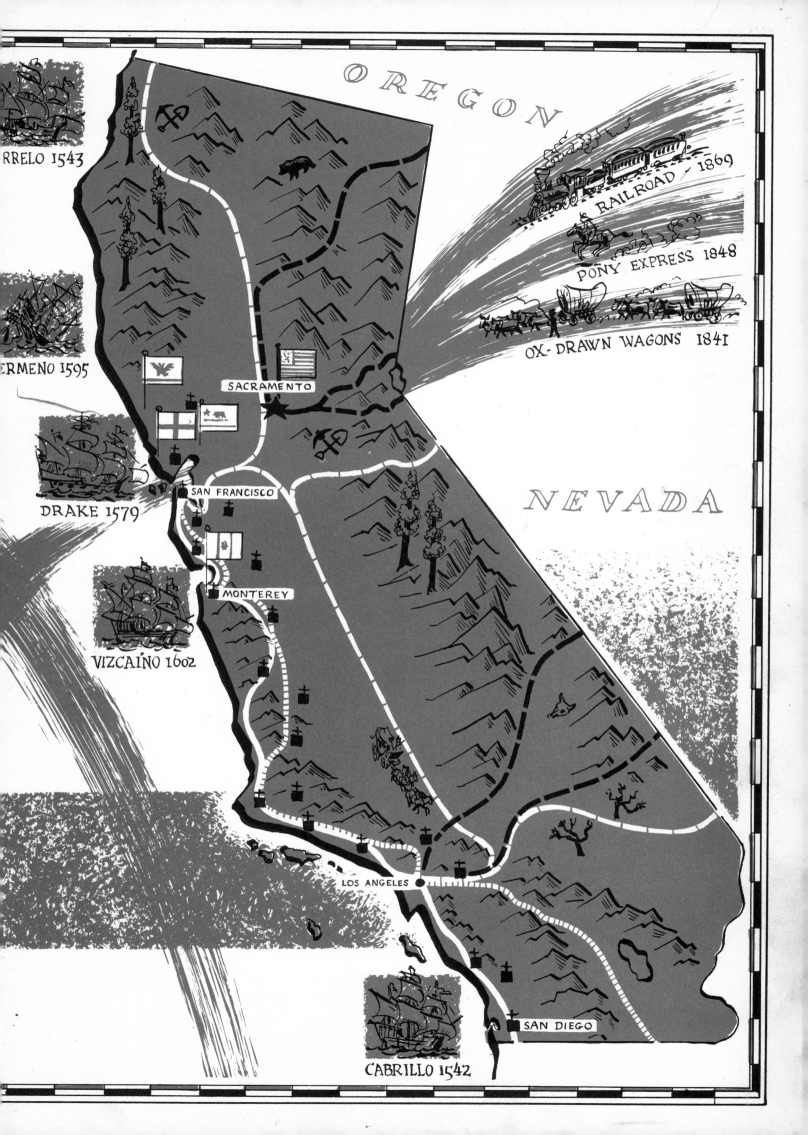

RRELO 1543

ERMENO 1595

DRAKE 1579

VIZCAÍNO 1602

CABRILLO 1542

OREGON

RAILROAD 1869

PONY EXPRESS 1848

OX-DRAWN WAGONS 1841

SACRAMENTO

NEVADA

SAN FRANCISCO

MONTEREY

LOS ANGELES

SAN DIEGO

*The Story of California*

# THE STORY OF
# CALIFORNIA

By Oscar Lewis

*Illustrated by John N. Barron*

GARDEN CITY BOOKS

*Garden City, N. Y.*

# CONTENTS

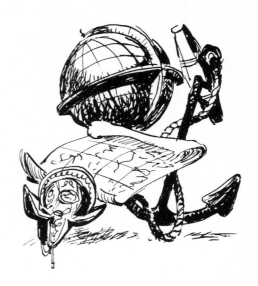

*Chapter I*

# DISCOVERY

WHEN, in the year 1492, three tiny ships, the *Santa Maria, Pinta,* and *Nina,* under the command of Christopher Columbus, left Spain and sailed westward across the ocean, there began a new and exciting phase of world history. For, after many weeks at sea, Columbus landed on one of the islands of the West Indies. There he raised the flag of Spain and claimed the new lands for King Ferdinand and Queen Isabella.

The voyage of Columbus ushered in a period of discovery and exploration and colonization that was to continue for well over three centuries. During that time the two great continents of North and South America, and the islands that lay off their shores, became known to the people of Europe. Soon large numbers of them were each year leaving their old homes and settling in the New World.

Not long after Columbus first crossed the Atlantic, other explorers, their ships flying the flags of Spain or Portugal or England, set out for the new lands. These sailed far to the north and south and explored thousands of miles of coastline. From time to time their captains went ashore and claimed the territory for their sovereigns. The first ships were followed by many others. These carried soldiers to conquer the natives, and colonists and supplies to found settlements there.

One of the first European nations to establish outpost colonies in the New World was Spain. In 1519 the Spanish king sent a skillful warrior, Hernando Cortez, with an army of two hundred soldiers to Mexico. That country was then ruled by a clever and resourceful people called the Aztecs. Their capital, Mexico City, with its temples and other fine buildings, had been in existence for hundreds of years. On this ancient stronghold of the

Aztecs, Cortez and his men advanced, and after a brief and bloody battle they captured it. Soon they had gained control of all Mexico.

Cortez, who had been named viceroy of New Spain, then sent out a number of expeditions to explore the conquered territory. One party, which he himself led, made its way to the west coast of Mexico and in small boats crossed to the peninsula of Lower California and founded a colony there. After only a few years, however, this colony was abandoned.

Meantime Cortez had heard from the Indians stories that seven great cities, rich in gold and other treasure, were located far to the north. Search for this prize, which became known as the Kingdom of Cibola, got promptly under way and continued for many years. Although the cities of Cibola were never found, the time and effort spent in the hunt for them were not wasted. For, because of this great search, much of the area that now makes up the southwestern part of the United States was explored far earlier than would otherwise have been the case.

One such expedition, led by Francisco Vásquez de Coronado, set off for the north in 1540. Coronado's party numbered well over a thousand men. Three hundred of them were trained Spanish soldiers armed with spears, lances, and the primitive firearms of the time. For two long years this expedition made its way through the mountains and deserts, searching for the Kingdom of Cibola. Although they came on many pueblos occupied by the Indians of the Southwest, some of them quite large and handsome, none contained the treasure for which they were looking. After passing over much of what is now Arizona and New Mexico and proceeding as far north as present-day Kansas, the disappointed searchers returned to Mexico City.

While Coronado's party was absent on this quest, a new Spanish viceroy, Antonio de Mendoza, fitted out a second expedition, this one to travel by sea and explore the unknown coastline to the northwest. Under the command of a skilled navigator named Juan Rodríguez Cabrillo, this group set off from the west coast of Mexico in two tiny vessels, the *San Salvador* and the *Victoria*. Rounding the tip of the peninsula of Lower California, the ships proceeded northward and, on September 28, 1542, dropped anchor in a pleasant bay. This harbor Cabrillo named San Miguel. Today we call it San Diego. His party, so far as is known, were the first Europeans to set foot on California soil.

After a brief stay there, the little ships again headed northward while Cabrillo explored the coastline and conferred names on islands, capes, bays,

and other places. All went well during the first weeks of the voyage. However, winter presently came on, and after rounding Point Conception, which juts out into the sea some 220 miles north of San Diego, a series of storms were encountered.

Meantime the commander, Cabrillo, had met with an accident during a stop at one of the islands in the Santa Barbara Channel, severely injuring his leg and shoulder. Despite this accident, he insisted on continuing his explorations to the unknown north. The ships pressed on, reaching Monterey and some distance beyond before continuous storms forced them to turn south again. During that long and rough voyage the commander's condition grew steadily worse. When the *San Salvador* and *Victoria,* badly battered and with their provisions all but exhausted, dropped anchor off one of the islands in the Santa Barbara Channel, the brave Cabrillo died and was buried there.

This tragedy, however, did not cause the expedition to be abandoned. Under the command of Cabrillo's chief pilot, Bartolomé Ferrelo, the tiny vessels once more headed northward. Storms continued to make progress slow and difficult. For one long period violent winds blew the ships far to sea. Their crews, with their food nearly gone and many suffering from a painful disease called scurvy, despaired of ever again seeing land. Nonetheless they reached what is now the northern boundary of California before they finally turned back.

Weeks later, after having faced many perils and hardships, the little ships returned safely to the Mexican port from which they had sailed many months before. Cabrillo and his men had made the coast of California known to the world.

*Chapter II*

# DRAKE AND THE *GOLDEN HIND*

AFTER Cabrillo's ships left the shores of California, more than thirty years passed before another vessel appeared in these remote waters. This next visitor flew the flag, not of Spain, but of England, and she was commanded by one of the most noted sailors of that seafaring nation. His name was Francis Drake.

In order to explain how Drake happened to bring his ship, the *Golden Hind,* to this faraway coast, it is necessary to tell something of the beginnings of that memorable voyage. Spain and England were then at peace and both had many ships engaged in trade throughout the known world. The Spanish ships of the period, high, slow-moving craft known as galleons, made regular trips to America and the Orient, returning laden with silks, spices, jewels, and other valuable goods, including gold and silver. Because of the treasure they carried, these galleons were rich prizes, and adventurous English seamen, called freebooters, roamed the seas in search of them. When one was sighted they attacked it, killing the crew and making off with the cargo it carried.

Drake was one of this group of English freebooters and by far the most daring and successful. In 1571, when he was about thirty, he led a raid against the prosperous Spanish settlements on the Isthmus of Panama. While there he saw for the first time the waters of the Pacific, and he resolved that some day he would lead an expedition into that ocean. This opportunity came six years later. In 1577 he set sail from the English port of Plymouth in command of a little fleet numbering five vessels.

Crossing the broad expanse of the Atlantic and sailing down the coast of South America, his ships entered the Straits of Magellan—which had

been discovered by Ferdinand Magellan half a century earlier—and, after a perilous seventeen-day journey, emerged safely into the waters of the Pacific.

Thus far all had gone well. Soon, however, many trials and dangers were met with. For although the ocean into which they had sailed bore the name Pacific—which means peaceful—it proved far from peaceful for Drake and his men. From the time they entered it they battled an almost continuous series of storms. One of the five ships was engulfed in a tremendous sea and sank with all on board. The others were driven far apart and three of them, having lost all contact with their leader, turned about and returned to England.

Drake, however, was not discouraged. In command now of the one remaining ship, the *Golden Hind,* he sailed up the west coast of South America, bound for the rich Spanish settlements in Peru, Panama, and Mexico. Sailing boldly into one port after another, he surprised their inhabitants and looted them of their treasure. One rich prize that fell to him and his men was a galleon named the *Cacafuego,* meaning "Spitfire." From it they captured many jewels and other valuables and more than twenty-five tons of silver bars from the mines of Peru.

Because the *Golden Hind* was presently loaded to capacity with the loot he had gathered, Drake made ready to return to England. However, by then he had been many months at sea and, before starting on the long voyage home, he searched for a safe spot where he could beach the little craft and clean its bottom which had become thickly encrusted with barnacles and other sea growth. On the lookout for a likely place to make these repairs, he continued up the coast to California, finally putting into a harbor somewhere in the vicinity of San Francisco Bay.

Precisely where Drake made his historic California landing has long been a matter of doubt. Some authorities state that it was at an inlet a few miles north of the Golden Gate, which is now known as Drake's Bay. Others believe that he entered San Francisco Bay itself and refitted his vessel somewhere on its shores. In any event, he remained there for several weeks while the needed repairs were made. The Indians of the region proved friendly and peaceable, and they were much interested in this strange craft and its white-skinned crew that had appeared among them.

On his part, Drake found the country attractive, abounding in game and other wild life. When he sailed away in July 1579, he left attached to a post on a nearby hill a plate of brass. On its surface were engraved in crude letters the date of his arrival and a statement that he claimed these lands, which he called Nova Albion—that is, New England—in the name of his sovereign, Queen Elizabeth.

It is interesting to know that this plate, after being all but forgotten for more than three and a half centuries, has in recent times been much discussed. For in 1936 there was picked up at a point not far from Drake's Bay a small metal plaque, which on being cleaned was found to bear an inscription very like the one Drake had left behind in 1579. Whether or not this is the very plate Drake affixed to "a faire great post" so long ago is not yet known with complete certainty. However, nearly every authority who has examined it has pronounced it genuine. It is now preserved in the Bancroft Library at the University of California and is looked on as a historic relic of great interest and importance.

After leaving the California coast, the *Golden Hind* crossed the Pacific and Indian oceans and rounded the Cape of Good Hope at the southern tip of Africa. Then, many months later, the little craft triumphantly dropped anchor at its starting place, Plymouth Harbor, having sailed entirely around the world.

*Chapter III*

# THE MANILA GALLEONS

DURING this early period Spain's trade with the Orient was carried on in ships called Manila galleons. These, starting from the Philippine Islands, sailed over the Pacific Ocean to the west coast of Mexico. Their cargos of silks, spices, jewels, and similar products were then transported on muleback across Mexico and loaded on other ships which took them to the Spanish peninsula.

The longest and most difficult part of this journey was that which lay between Manila and the Mexican port of Acapulco. It was a voyage that usually lasted from six to eight months. For, in making the crossing from west to east, the heavily laden galleons did not travel a direct course. Instead, they swung far to the north, sailing almost to the shores of Japan before turning toward America. This was done for two reasons. First, because by choosing that route, the severe tropical storms could be avoided. Second, it was only by sailing far to the north that the trade winds, blowing steadily from west to east, were met with. Once these were encountered, they sped the little ships toward their home port of Acapulco.

But this Great Circle Route, as it was called, also had its drawbacks. For the distance that had to be traveled was very long. The result was that before the journeys were ended the supplies of food and water often ran low and all on board suffered severely.

It was to find a place somewhere along the route where the voyage could be broken, new supplies taken on board, and repairs made to the ships themselves, that the next explorations of the California coast were undertaken. On their west-east crossings the galleons usually first sighted the mainland in the vicinity of Cape Mendocino, the bold headland that

15

lies about midway between San Francisco Bay and the present northern boundary of the state. It was the hope that a safe harbor could be discovered somewhere near that point.

Accordingly, the masters of the galleons were ordered to be on the lookout for a suitable stopping place as they sailed down the coast toward Acapulco. One of the first men selected for this task was Sebastián Rodríguez Cermeno, the commander of a 200-ton galleon, the *San Agustin.* Sailing from Manila in the summer of 1595, Cermeno first sighted California near Cape Mendocino and proceeded down the coast looking for such a harbor. However, on his first stop, at a small inlet to the north of San Francisco Bay, a violent storm came up. The *San Agustin* was driven far up on the beach and had to be abandoned there, a total wreck.

Following that disaster, it was decided to send an expedition from Mexico to continue the search for a harbor. Thus in the spring of 1602 three vessels, under the command of Sebastián Vizcaíno, set forth. Making their way slowly up the coast of the Lower California peninsula, they some six months later dropped anchor in the bay of San Diego, which Cabrillo had discovered about sixty years earlier. Vizcaíno was favorably impressed

with this harbor and wrote the viceroy that it would be an ideal stopping place for the Manila galleons.

Continuing to the north, Vizcaíno made frequent stops, not only on the mainland but on the islands lying in the Santa Barbara Channel. Everywhere he was met by groups of friendly natives, from whom he obtained food in return for gifts of cloth and other trinkets. Rounding Point Conception, the ships proceeded northward and, toward the end of 1602, sailed into a second spacious harbor. This, which the commander named Monterey in honor of the Spanish viceroy, the Count of Monterey, also aroused his enthusiasm.

In a letter to the Spanish king, written from that port on December 28, 1602, Vizcaíno stated that "this harbor of Monterey is . . . well situated in point of latitude for that which His Majesty intends to do for the protection and security of ships coming from the Philippines. In it may be repaired the damages which they may have sustained, for there is a great extent of pine forest from which to obtain masts and yards." He added that "the land is thickly peopled by Indians and is very fertile, its climate and the quality of the soil resembling Castile, and any seed grown there will give fruit, and there are extensive lands fair for pasturage, and many kinds of animals and birds . . ."

Vizcaíno's discovery of Monterey Bay was the high point of his expedition. From there he sent back to Mexico the smallest of his three ships, bearing those of his party who had become sick or disabled. In the others,

including his flagship, the *San Diego,* he continued up the coast. By then, however, the winter storms had set in and progress was slow and difficult. Nonetheless, the little vessels pressed on to a point some distance beyond Cape Mendocino before heavy winds and fog, and the sickness of all but a few of the men, caused them at length to turn south again.

The long voyage back to the Mexican port from which the little expedition had started was a trying ordeal for all. The weather continued rough, the supply of food was both scanty and in bad condition, and all but a few of the crew were suffering from scurvy. When the *San Diego* and its companion ship finally reached Mazatlan at the end of their eight months' voyage, only five men were strong enough to go ashore and get supplies and help for their companions.

Their sufferings, however, were soon forgotten in their gratitude at having reached home safely. As soon as he was able, Vizcaíno hastened to Mexico City, where he was received with honor by the viceroy and congratulated on the success of his voyage. Both he and Father Ascension, the Spanish priest who had accompanied him on the journey, urged that a colony be established at the harbor of Monterey. This, they stated, would serve not only as a safe stopping place for the Manila galleons but would be a means of holding California for the Spanish crown and permit converting the natives to Christianity.

As it happened, however, well over a century and a half were to pass before the plan they recommended was carried out.

*Chapter IV*

# THE TRAIL-BREAKERS

DURING the many years that passed between Vizcaíno's visit in 1602 and the establishment of the first settlements in California, much had happened elsewhere on the continent. In 1607 the first party of English colonists to settle in the New World landed at Jamestown in Virginia. Thirteen years later, in 1620, the *Mayflower* deposited the Pilgrims at Plymouth Rock.

After another half century had passed, the explorer, La Salle, set off from the colonies the French had founded along the St. Lawrence River and, following the course of the Mississippi to its mouth on the Gulf of Mexico, claimed the great interior valley for his king. Then, toward the middle of the eighteenth century, yet another European nation laid claim to a part of the continent. Far to the north, a party of Russian fur hunters crossed the narrow waters from Siberia and established a colony on the coast of Alaska.

The Spanish, meantime, had not been idle. Under the leadership of a resourceful priest named Father Kino, a series of missions had been founded in present-day Arizona and in the Mexican state of Sonora. Kino urged the authorities at Mexico City to extend these outposts to the California coast and thereby strengthen the Spanish hold on that region. At length he was able to convince the highest Spanish official of the colony, José de Gálvez, of the wisdom of this.

Accordingly, early in 1769, two sturdy ships, the *San Carlos* and the *San Antonio,* both well supplied with men and provisions, set sail from a port on the west coast of Mexico and headed north. Their purpose was to found a settlement on the bay of Monterey, which Vizcaíno had discovered more than a hundred and sixty years earlier and of which he had written with so much enthusiasm.

At the same time a second expedition was organized and sent north. This one, which traveled overland, was commanded by an able soldier, Don Gaspar de Portolá. With him was Father Junípero Serra, the Spanish priest who was to become the founder of the group of missions soon to be established in the new land.

The two parties, one coming by sea and the other by land, met at San Diego. There Portolá laid out the plan of a military station, called a presidio, and Father Serra busied himself founding the first California mission. Soon, however, Portolá and his men pushed on to the north, his purpose to locate Monterey Bay and set up a permanent colony there. They, the first party of white men to travel by land up the coast, found the journey a long and difficult one.

Arriving at last on the Monterey peninsula, they failed to recognize it as the spot described by Vizcaíno. Accordingly, they continued northward and, early in November 1769, reached a spot on the coast a few miles to

the south of the Golden Gate. While they were camped there, a group of hunters, looking for deer or other animals to replenish their supply of food, climbed the hills to the east. On reaching their crest, they looked down on a great expanse of water stretching far to the north and south. They had discovered San Francisco Bay.

Portolá then led his men, weary from their six months' march through the wilds, back to San Diego. The following spring, however, he returned to Monterey, and this time Father Serra accompanied him. There Portolá set about building a fort and quarters for his soldiers, while the priest made ready to establish a second California mission near by. Thus the purposes for which the expeditions had been organized were at last accomplished.

During the next several years a number of other missions were founded and parties of soldiers explored much of the coast that lay between San Diego and the bay of San Francisco. However, but little of what the colonists needed could be produced locally, and for most of their supplies they had to depend on the ships sent up from Mexico, which arrived only at long intervals. It became clear that, if the new missions and presidios were to prosper, a faster and easier means of communication with the home country must be found.

Accordingly, a search was begun to locate an overland route by which needed provisions could be brought to the new settlements from Sonora, the northernmost of the Mexican provinces. The man chosen to undertake that task was a resourceful frontier soldier name Juan Bautista de Anza. His party, which set forth early in 1774, included twenty mounted soldiers, numerous horses and cattle, and a number of herdsmen to drive them. They faced a long and difficult journey. For their route passed over rugged mountain ranges, many miles of waterless desert, and involved a crossing of the wide Colorado River.

Nonetheless they eventually got through to the newly founded San Gabriel Mission in southern California, where they were welcomed with joy by the padres. After only a few days there, the tireless leader continued on up the coast to Monterey, then made his way back to the town of Tubac, his starting place. He had been gone less than five months. Yet during that time he had traveled well over two thousand miles, by far the greatest part of it through unexplored wilderness.

Having proved that it was possible to supply the remote California settlements by land, Anza was chosen to organize a second and far larger expedition and to lead it over the route he had discovered. This party, consisting not only of soldiers but also of many men, women, and children,

who were to settle in the new land, left Tubac late in 1775 and reached San Gabriel on January 4 of the following year.

This time Anza's chief purpose was to found a mission and presidio on the shores of the great harbor far to the north, which Portolá's men had discovered six years earlier. Accordingly, he led his party up the coast to the shores of San Francisco Bay, and there he selected the sites of a presidio and a mission. These were dedicated and the construction of the buildings was begun later that year, the presidio on September 17, and the mission on October 9.

Thus, largely because of Anza's efforts, Spain's hold on its remote province of California was at last made secure.

23

*Chapter V*

# THE MISSIONS AND RANCHOS

WITH the founding of the first Spanish settlements, California entered a new and interesting period of its history, one that was to last for close to three quarters of a century.

As in Spain's other New World possessions, some of which had been established more than two hundred years earlier, the task of governing and developing the colony was placed in the hands of two groups that had been sent out from the homeland for that purpose. These were the soldiers and the missionaries, and each had their own duties to perform.

It was the responsibility of the soldiers to see that order was maintained and that the missions and other settlements were protected from attacks by the native Indians or by raiding parties of other nations. For that purpose four military posts, or presidios, were established: at San Diego, Santa Barbara, Monterey, and San Francisco Bay. At each was erected a fort, built in the form of a rectangle. Its outer walls were made of adobe bricks; that is, the native soil to which grass and twigs were added to give more strength. A number of small, muzzle-loading cannon were mounted on the tops of the walls.

Near several of the presidios, and at various other places, towns, or pueblos, were founded. There the settlers and their families lived, and for their use large tracts of land were set aside near by, on which they grew their crops and raised their herds of horses, cattle, and sheep.

The third type of settlement established by the Spaniards in their new province was the missions. These were under the control of a religious order, the Franciscans, and their purpose was to convert the Indians to Christianity and to train them in the ways of civilization. Some converts were taught

24

to plant and harvest crops and to care for the mission herds. Others learned simple trades, as carpenters, blacksmiths, tanners of leather, millers, masons, and the like.

The missions were long the largest and most active settlements in the province. Beginning with the establishment of their first outpost at San Diego in 1769, the industrious Franciscans rapidly founded others until by the end of the century their number had reached eighteen. Later three more were added, making twenty-one in all. These were spaced at intervals from San Diego to Sonoma, a distance of more than five hundred miles. Hence travelers up and down the coast could stop each night at one or another of them, where they were always made welcome by the padres and their Indian converts.

During the period of their greatest activity, from about 1775 to the early 1800s, many of the missions were large and flourishing communities. At each, the chief building was the mission itself, a sturdy, thick-walled structure put up by the Indians under the direction of their teachers. Usually a steeple or bell tower rose above its tiled roof and the interior walls were decorated with brightly colored paintings of religious scenes.

Close to the mission, and often connected with it by covered colonnades, were the rooms of the padres and the shops in which the native artisans worked. Early-day visitors were much impressed by the variety and quality of the articles turned out at these shops. One traveler, during a stay of several days at the San Gabriel Mission, observed groups of Indians

making bricks and tiles, tanning hides, and baking bread, while others were working with wood or iron. At the same time yet other groups were cultivating the nearby fields and still others, called *vaqueros,* watched over the big mission herds grazing on the surrounding ranges.

The period of the missions, one of the most colorful in California's history, lasted a little more than sixty years. It came to an end in 1833 when the Mexican government—Mexico having gained its independence from Spain some twelve years earlier—passed what was known as the Secularization Act. This deprived the missions of their lands and caused their hundreds of Indian converts to drift away. Some of the natives gathered in the towns and villages of the province while others rejoined their wild tribesmen in the mountains and valleys of the interior.

Then began yet another era in the history of the province, that of the great cattle ranches. Although during the period when California was ruled by Spain certain grants of land had been made to individuals—usually to former soldiers who had served out their terms at one or another of the presidios—the practice did not become widespread until after the passage of the Secularization Act. Thereafter many such grants were made. Because the country still had but few settlers and millions of acres of fertile farming and grazing lands were unoccupied, these grants were always of generous size. The smallest area allotted to any applicant was one square league, and many were more than ten times as big.

As the missions had been earlier, these great ranchos became favorite stopping places for those traveling up or down the coast. Their owners were genial hosts, and any stranger who happened to pass that way was sure of a hearty welcome and an invitation to stay as long as he liked. One such wayfarer who journeyed up the coast in the early 1840s recorded in his diary that at each stop he was furnished with a fresh horse on which to ride to the next rancho, and that a supply of silver coins was laid out in his bedroom, to which he was expected to help himself should he be in need of funds.

The fact that the ranchos were spaced far apart, and that usually only rough trails led from one to the other, did not prevent the owners and their families from paying frequent visits to their distant neighbors. They were a happy, carefree people, who liked nothing better than to gather at one or another of the haciendas, as their ranch houses were called, and there spend several days feasting, dancing, and performing difficult feats of horsemanship, for all were skilled riders. They were able to leave their ranchos thus unattended for considerable periods because they raised on them only horses

and cattle, which roamed the valleys and foothills of their property, needing little care.

Once a year, however, usually in the late spring, the big herds were rounded up and the young horses and cattle branded. At the same time some of the animals were slaughtered. Their hides were carried to Monterey, Santa Barbara, or other points on the coast, where they were exchanged with the masters of the Yankee trading ships for clothing, firearms, musical instruments, jewelry, and many other articles brought out from New England in the little trading vessels.

*Chapter VI*

# THE COMING OF FOREIGNERS

DURING the first years after the Spaniards established their missions, presidios, and pueblos, the ships of other nations appeared in the harbors of the province only at long intervals. As time passed, however, such visits grew more frequent. Some of the earliest of these, small sailing vessels that flew the flag of Russia, made their way down the coast from distant Alaska, where, as we have seen, the Russians had founded fur-trading posts in the 1780s.

These ships visited California waters for two reasons. One was to hunt for sea otters, which were then numerous in the off-shore waters, and the fine furs of which had a ready market in the Orient. Most of the skins were sold at the Chinese port of Canton, where they brought upwards of $100 each.

The second reason why the Russian ships made the long voyage down from Alaska was to obtain supplies of grain, corn, and other crops, for these products could not be successfully grown in their cold northern settlements. It was for the purpose of raising such supplies themselves that the Russians, in 1812, founded a colony on the California coast. This was located at Fort Ross, some sixty miles north of San Francisco Bay. There they built a group of sturdy buildings laid out in the form of a square and enclosed by a high fence for protection against attack. Outside this stockade orchards were set out and fields were planted to grain, potatoes, and other crops.

The Californians were at first much disturbed at the establishment of this Russian colony, which was only a day's journey from the northern-most of their own settlements, that at Sonoma. However, they had no real

cause for alarm, for Fort Ross failed to flourish, and in 1841 the Russians sold their property there and withdrew to the north.

The man who purchased their belongings was Captain John A. Sutter. Captain Sutter, one of the most important and picturesque of the early residents of the province, had arrived in California in the summer of 1839 and settled in the Sacramento Valley. From the Mexican governor, Juan B. Alvarado, he obtained a grant of some 50,000 acres of the fertile land. There, with the help of the friendly Indians and a few frontiersmen who had drifted into the valley, he set about creating a colony, which he called New Helvetia after his native Switzerland. During the next few years hundreds of acres were planted to grain and other crops, while great herds of cattle roamed over the neighboring plains, watched over by Mexican *vaqueros* whom he hired for that purpose.

To serve as the headquarters for his inland empire, Sutter built, at a point on the American River where the city of Sacramento now stands, a settlement that became known far and wide as Sutter's Fort. This was a small town in itself, consisting of his own living quarters, storehouses, blacksmith and carpenter shops, and other structures. All were enclosed in a high wall made of adobe bricks and having at each of its four corners a tower in which cannons were mounted. It and its genial owner were destined to play a leading part in the dramatic events that were to take place in the colony during the next few years.

For, as time passed, this Mexican province on the west coast had come to arouse increasing interest on the far side of the continent, and each year greater numbers of citizens of the United States made their way there. Many of these came in the little whaling and trading ships of the day. During the late 1830s and early 1840s these vessels, sailing out of Salem and other New England ports, appeared with ever-increasing frequency off the coast.

The whalers stopped at San Diego, Monterey, San Francisco, and other ports in order to take on fresh supplies of food and water. The second class of vessels, the trading ships, brought out cargos of merchandise of various sorts. They sailed up and down the coast, making stops at numerous bays and inlets along the way. Everywhere they were warmly welcomed by residents of the area, in particular by those who lived on the big, lonely cattle ranches.

When the ranchers learned that a trading ship had arrived in the vicinity, they, together with their wives and children and employees, hurried to the landing place, often traveling many miles on horseback or in the crude ox-drawn carts that were their only vehicles. At the beach sailors took them in small boats and rowed them out to the ship, which was often anchored some distance from the shore. Upon arriving on board, they were taken into one of the vessel's cabins, which had been fitted up as a store, and there made their purchases.

Seldom were the goods the ranchers bought on these visits paid for in cash, for money of any kind was scarce in the California of that day. Instead, the ship-owners took in exchange the products of the country, chiefly hides and tallow, the first of which became known to the traders as "California banknotes." A graphic picture of what life was like aboard these Yankee trading ships is given in *Two Years Before the Mast,* which was first published in 1840. Its author, Richard Henry Dana, had as a youth in his early twenties spent many months as a seaman aboard one such ship. The story of his experiences has ever since been widely read because of the picture it gives of the California of that day.

However, not all those who arrived in the province during that period came by sea. American frontiersmen had for a generation or more been pushing westward across the Mississippi Valley and into the Rocky Mountain country, each year drawing closer to the Mexican possession on the far coast. In the van of these pioneers were the fur trappers. These sturdy

"mountain men," as they were called, yearly broke new trails throughout the West in their search for beaver and other fur-bearing animals that lived along the courses of the wilderness streams.

The first of these pathfinders to reach California was 27-year-old Jedediah Smith. In the spring of 1826 Smith, leading a party of seventeen men, set off from Great Salt Lake, and after a long and dangerous journey through the waterless wastes of the Southwest, reached the San Gabriel Mission in southern California some three months later.

This, however, was not Smith's only history-making journey. For, when he set out to return to Salt Lake, he led his men up the San Joaquin Valley and, in January of the next year, attempted a crossing of the towering Sierra Nevada range. Driven back by the deep snowdrifts on the upper ridges, he was forced to return to the valley. Some four months later, on May 20, 1827, he made a second attempt. This time, taking but two men, seven horses, and two mules to carry provisions, he managed after eight days of struggle to pass over the lofty summit and down to the sage-covered plains below.

He and his two companions were the first white men to cross over the Sierra. During the years that followed many thousands of others were to follow the trail he had broken.

*Chapter VII*

# THE BEAR FLAG

WHEN the early-day Yankee traders and seamen returned to their homes after visits to California, they had many tales to tell of the attractions of that distant land. Its climate, they reported, was mild, and so healthful that sickness was almost unknown. Moreover, the land was plentiful, the soil fertile, and in order to attract settlers the government officials at Monterey were deeding great areas of desirable countryside to those who applied, and on extremely generous terms. Some of these land grants, as they were called, were of more than 20,000 acres, and many were almost as large.

With such glowing accounts spreading throughout the east coast and across the Mississippi Valley, it was not long before groups began making plans to migrate to the new land and settle there. It was in the spring of 1841 that the first party of emigrants set off on that long and grueling journey. This company, numbering some seventy men, women, and children, and led by a young man named John Bidwell, started from the frontier settlement of Sapling Grove in present-day Kansas.

Knowing little of what route to follow or of what dangers might lie before them, they headed their horses, mules, and ox-drawn wagons toward the far coast. During the early part of their journey they had little difficulty, for they followed the well-marked trails of the fur traders as far as Great Salt Lake. Beyond that point, however, their troubles multiplied. Crossing the hot, sandy plains of what is now Nevada, both they and their animals suffered severely from the lack of food and water.

When at last they reached the base of the towering Sierra Nevada range, the Bidwell party faced a new and even greater danger. For by then winter was coming on and, should they be overtaken by snowstorms while crossing the lofty crest, they might all be trapped and perish. Nonetheless, they

33

pressed on and, passing over the summit, made their way safely down into the broad central valley below.

It was not long before this pioneer, trail-breaking emigrant group was followed by others. Nearly all got through safely, though most of them suffered severe privations, and occasional dangers, along the way. One large company, attempting a crossing of the Sierra dangerously late in the season, found themselves snowbound beside a mountain lake, and many perished before rescue parties could reach the camps of the survivors the following spring. These were members of the Donner Party, whose story is one of the most tragic in the annals of the early West.

Meanwhile the Mexican government at Mexico City, faced by many problems closer to home, was able to pay but little attention to its distant west coast possession. The California presidios, or forts, that had earlier been established were allowed to fall into ruin. Some were abandoned entirely, and at others the garrisons were reduced to a few soldiers, without proper arms or ammunition and most of them long unpaid.

By the beginning of the late 1840s it had become clear that the mother country's hold on the province could not be much longer maintained. It was widely believed, both in California and elsewhere, that the region must

soon be taken over by some other nation. Throughout the United States there was a strong feeling that it should not be allowed to fall under the control of a European power, and when rumors presently reached Washington that Great Britain was planning to seize the province, they aroused much uneasiness.

It was partly on that account that an exploring expedition, under the command of Captain John C. Frémont, set off for California in the spring of 1845. That was not Frémont's first visit to the west coast. The year previous, he had led a party into the Northwest as far as Fort Vancouver on the Columbia River and, on his return, had crossed into California and spent several weeks at Sutter's Fort before making his way home by a circuitous southern route.

Frémont's second stay in California was, however, to prove far more eventful than his first. For, on again reaching Sutter's Fort, he led his party, numbering some sixty men, toward the southwest and made camp on the crest of a hill called Gavalin Peak, only a few miles from the Mexican capital at Monterey. On being ordered by the authorities there to break camp and leave the province, Frémont refused to do so. Thereupon the Mexicans gathered a considerable number of mounted men at the base of the hill and

35

prepared to eject them by force. However, bloodshed was averted, for Frémont and his followers slipped away during the night and made their way
back to the Sacramento Valley, bound for Oregon.

But, after they had progressed some distance, they were overtaken by a
messenger who had been sent out from Washington bearing secret instruc-
tions for their leader. The result was that Frémont and his men turned about
and hastened back to Sutter's Fort. There he found that a group of American settlers, alarmed at reports that the Mexican authorities were preparing
to drive out all foreigners, were planning to take forceable possession of the
province and to set up an independent republic.

As a first step in that daring plan, a party of armed frontiersmen, led by
William B. Ide, appeared at Sonoma, the northernmost of the Mexican
settlements and, on July 14, 1846, made prisoners of several of its citizens,
including General Mariano Vallejo. Having taken possession of the town,
the group announced the formation of the Republic of California, and set
about making a flag for their new republic. Using such materials as were
at hand, they fashioned a crude emblem representing a grizzly bear outlined
in red against a white background, with under it the words "California Republic." It was because of this device that the Sonoma episode became
known in history as the Bear Flag Rebellion.

Following the capture of Sonoma, Captain Frémont took command of
the revolting forces and prepared to meet the expected attacks of the Mexicans. Such encounters failed to take place, however. While both sides were

preparing for battle, word reached the province that war between the United States and Mexico had broken out some three months earlier. On July 7, 1846, American naval forces landed and, without opposition, took possession of the Mexican capital at Monterey, raising there the American flag.

Although during the months that followed Mexican forces, particularly in the southern part of the province, resisted the invaders, such "battles" as were fought resulted in little bloodshed on either side. Then, with the signing of the Treaty of Guadalupe Hidalgo on February 2, 1848, the southern republic formally ceded California to the United States.

*Chapter VIII*

# GOLD!

AT almost exactly the same time the former Mexican province became a part of the United States, an event took place there that was soon to draw to California tens of thousands of adventurers, not only from the east coast but from many parts of the world.

The story of how this came about forms one of the most dramatic chapters in California's history. Toward the end of 1847 Captain Sutter, busy with plans for the further development of his ranch and trading post in the Sacramento Valley, and needing lumber for additional warehouses and other buildings, decided to construct a sawmill.

Accordingly, he assembled a crew of workmen and, with a young Yankee named James Marshall in charge, sent them into the foothills of the Sierra to choose a site and put up the mill. The spot they selected was in a little valley on the south fork of the American River, some forty miles to the northeast of Sutter's Fort. There Marshall and his helpers worked throughout the winter building the mill and digging a ditch designed to carry off the water after it had passed over the wheel.

Work on this project was well advanced when, on the morning of January 24, 1848, Marshall chanced to notice some glittering particles at the bottom of the partially completed millrace. He stooped and gathered up a few of these, for their bright yellow color led him to think that they might be gold. He applied to them such simple tests as he knew, and then, not yet convinced that they were really gold, carried them to Sutter's Fort and showed them to his employer. There Captain Sutter submitted them to further tests, which proved beyond doubt that they were indeed fragments of the precious metal.

Sutter was not altogether pleased at this discovery. For he foresaw that, should word get about that gold had been found on the site of his sawmill, the workmen would spend their time gathering it and his mill would remain uncompleted. He accompanied Marshall up into the foothills and, after gathering still other particles from the bottom of the ditch, obtained a promise from the others to say nothing of the discovery until the mill was finished and in operation.

But exciting news of that sort could not be long kept secret. Two of the workmen presently slipped away to Sacramento, the settlement that had sprung up beside the river, adjacent to Sutter's Fort. With them they carried specimens of the gold, which they exhibited to various persons in the town.

Among those who thus learned of the discovery was Samuel Brannan, an energetic San Francisco merchant who had recently established a branch store at Sacramento. After paying a visit to the foothills and assuring himself that gold was abundant in the streams there, he returned to San Francisco, holding aloft a well-filled leather bag and shouting dramatically, "Gold! Gold in the American River!"

This of course aroused high excitement throughout the town, and many prepared to hurry to the gold fields and gather in a share of the treasure. Once started, the news spread like wildfire: to San Jose, Monterey, and the towns to the south. Merchants closed their shops and innkeepers their hotels, carpenters left their benches and ranchers abandoned their herds, while all headed for the scene of the discovery. The gold rush was on!

These, however, were merely forerunners of the great stampede that followed. For news of the discovery presently reached the east coast, and when, on December 5, 1848, President Polk in his message to Congress confirmed that gold was abundant in the new possession, it everywhere aroused intense excitement.

Beginning early the following spring and continuing through the year 1849 and much of 1850, a horde of gold hunters poured into California. They

came from all points of the compass. Overland parties, following the trails first broken by the fur hunters, set off from frontier settlements in the Mississippi Valley as soon as the grasses were tall enough to provide food for the animals that drew their heavily loaded wagons. During the height of the movement so many were heading westward over the plains and deserts and mountains that at night the glow of their countless campfires could be seen for miles.

Those who came by this route were, however, only a part of the mighty invasion. An even greater number made the journey by sea. All along the Atlantic Coast and Gulf of Mexico scores of ships were fitted out, and, loaded to capacity with miners and their supplies, set off to the new Eldorado. Many made the months-long voyage round the southern tip of South America. Others landed at Panama, where their passengers hurried across the narrow isthmus and re-embarked on ships that took them up the west coast. Nor were these all. Numerous other vessels were hastening toward the gold fields, from England, France, and other countries of Europe, from Australia, China, and elsewhere.

This sudden arrival of thousands upon thousands of newcomers, nearly all of them energetic and adventurous young men, speedily transformed the once quiet Mexican province. Within a few months the sleepy village on the shore of San Francisco Bay had grown to a teeming city, and the bay itself was crowded with hundreds of idle ships, the crews of which had deserted and hurried off to the mines. Sacramento, Stockton, Marysville, and

other towns in the central valley grew almost as fast, for these became the supply and trading centers for the camps that were springing up everywhere in the Sierra foothills.

It was, however, in the gold country itself that the greatest changes took place. For in their search for the precious metal the prospectors overran the entire region from the Oregon border to the southern limits of the Sierra range. First scores and then hundreds of camps were established. Some were along the lower reaches of the streams as they flowed through the foothills toward the valley. Others were in remote canyons high up toward the summit of the mountains. How the miners fared was largely a matter of luck. Some were fortunate enough to locate extremely rich claims and in a few days or weeks washed out many thousands of dollars worth of gold. Others had to be content with a far smaller yield from their labors, and yet others found nothing at all.

But although all but a few of the Argonauts were disappointed in their dreams of easy wealth, the gold rush had a profound effect on the destinies of California. For it drew to the new land many thousands of sturdy, ambitious young men, and thus prepared the way for the great state that was soon to come into being.

*Chapter IX*

# THE THIRTY-FIRST STATE

WHEN California became a part of the United States early in 1848, it was placed under the command of a military governor who was assigned to rule over the new possession until Congress could pass an act taking it into the union as a territory or a state. Meantime, as we have seen, the gold rush had brought many thousands into the country, the great majority of whom were citizens of the United States. These newcomers were naturally anxious to be governed, not by military law, but by regularly elected civilian officials, as had been the case in their former homes.

The result was that petitions were regularly sent to Washington urging that steps be taken to permit the holding of elections at which executives, judges, law-enforcement officers, and others could be chosen and begin to serve. In response to these requests, the military governor, General Bennett Riley, presently called for an election to choose delegates to a state constitutional convention, to meet at Monterey in the summer of 1849. This election was duly held, and on August 1 of that year a group of forty-eight men, representing communities in all parts of the state, assembled in one of the adobe buildings at the old Spanish-Mexican capital.

For more than two months the delegates busied themselves drawing up a constitution for the new state, fixing its boundaries to the north, south, and east, and specifying how it was to be governed. When their labors were completed, a second election was held at which the new constitution was adopted by an overwhelming majority of the voters. The document was then sent to Washington for approval by the Congress and the formal admission into the union of the state of California.

Meanwhile the citizens, not waiting for word from the national capital that their application for statehood had been approved, set about putting

43

their new constitution into effect. A governor and other officials were chosen and took office, and the first legislature met at San Jose in December 1849. The new government had begun to function.

It was not until months later that Congress got around to approving the admission of the state, and the bill did not receive President Fillmore's signature until September 9, 1850. There was a further delay of a month and a half before word of this action reached California. When the news arrived, however, it was everywhere greeted with rejoicing. In numerous towns and camps parades were held, speeches delivered, and cannons and other firearms fired as the residents expressed their joy. California had become the thirty-first state of the union.

By then the excitement of the gold rush had already passed its crest. The thousands of miners, working with their pans and rockers and sluice boxes, had washed most of the gold from the beds of the mountain and foothill streams. When these placers, as they were called, were one by one exhausted, most of the inhabitants of the camps drifted away. Some returned to their old homes in the East or elsewhere. Many others, however, chose to stay on and become permanent residents of the new state.

To be sure, gold mining remained one of California's leading industries for more than a quarter century longer. But the methods used in this later period were quite different from those employed in 1849 and the early 1850s. For much of the metal, instead of being in the form of nuggets or flakes that could be easily gathered, was embedded in solid rock. To recover this, a complicated process, known as quartz mining, had to be employed. This involved the building of stamp mills at which the quartz was reduced to powder and the gold extracted, and the sinking of shafts beneath the surface to reach rich veins of gold-bearing rock that lay underground.

Yet another method, called hydraulic mining, was widely used during the late 1850s and for some years thereafter. By this process, water was brought down from higher in the mountains and, flowing under great pressure through iron pipes, was played on gold-bearing hillsides, washing them down into long sluices where the metal was extracted. However, by this method so much earth and gravel were washed into the streams that their beds became clogged for many miles below, causing them to overflow their banks and flood the fields of the farmers who had settled along their courses. The result was that in the late 1870s the state legislature passed a law forbidding the dumping of such material into the streams. This brought the hydraulic mining era to an end.

By then agriculture and stock raising had supplanted mining as the state's most important industries. As we have seen, the raising of cattle had been the first, and indeed almost the only, gainful occupation of the early Spanish and Mexican residents. The immense herds of the mission fathers and of the ranch owners had roamed over the coastal hills from San Diego to San Francisco, and a brisk trade in hides and tallow had been carried on with the Yankee trading ships. During the gold rush so many thousands were drawn to the towns and camps of the north that the ranchers in the lower part of the state—which was long known as the "cow country"—shared in the general prosperity by driving their herds north and selling them, at high prices, to the miners.

As gold production declined, more and more miners each year abandoned their worked-out claims and, settling on the fertile valley and foothill lands, put them under cultivation. Soon a large variety of crops were being raised. In the area to the north and south of San Francisco Bay some of these pioneers set out vineyards, thus beginning the great wine industry that has ever since flourished. Elsewhere many varieties of fruit trees were planted, and fields were sown to grain, barley, and other crops.

From the early 1860s onward the growing of wheat became the major industry in the big central valleys of the Sacramento and the San Joaquin. There great ranches, some of them 20,000 acres or more in extent, were yearly planted to that crop, and during the next two decades vast quantities of California wheat were shipped to the markets of the world. Something of this interesting—and important—"Epic of the Wheat" will be told in a later chapter.

*Chapter X*

# THE END OF ISOLATION

WHEN, nearly two centuries ago, the first parties of Spanish settlers arrived in California, the complaint they most frequently made about their new home was that it was so far removed from other inhabited areas. This feeling among residents that they were cut off by great distances from the rest of the civilized world continued not only throughout the period when the province was ruled by Spain and Mexico but after it had become a part of the United States. And for many years thereafter.

Moreover, the early-day Californians had good reason to feel as they did. They were separated by thousands of miles from their former homes, and communication with the outer world was both slow and uncertain. This was particularly true throughout the Spanish and Mexican periods. For then the residents had to depend for news from the outside on a government ship that once a year made a trip up from the west coast of Mexico, or on the whaling and trading vessels that appeared at intervals at one or another of the harbors.

Even after the territory was annexed to the United States and the gold discovery had drawn thousands to its shores, this same complaint was still often heard. The mails were so slow that often four or five months passed before a reply could be received to a letter sent to a correspondent on the other side of the continent.

To be sure, just as the gold rush was getting under way, the national government entered into contracts with the owners of two pioneer steamship lines to carry the mails between the two coasts. The ships of one line operated between New York and New Orleans and Panama, and those of the other from Panama north to San Francisco. In the beginning the ships on the Pacific run made one round trip a month. Later, however, other steamers were added, and by the early 1850s there were weekly sailings in both directions. Although for years the little vessels were crowded to capacity on every trip, with many passengers having to sleep on deck, in the corridors below, or even on the tables in the dining salon, this was long the quickest and easiest way of traveling between the two coasts.

Meantime steps were being taken to provide better means of crossing over the hundreds of miles of mountains and desert that lay between California and the outpost settlements in the Mississippi Valley. As we have seen, the first Argonauts made the journey afoot or on horseback, with

their belongings carried in cumbersome, high-wheeled wagons called prairie schooners.

Then in 1858 the government made a contract with the Butterfield Overland Mail Company for the regular transportation of mails between a town in western Missouri and San Francisco. This route swung far to the south, thereby avoiding passing over the rugged Sierra Nevada range and, entering California close to the Mexican border, continued upward to the bay. The distance from starting point to destination was well over 2,500 miles, and the lumbering, horse-drawn stages, traveling day and night and in all sorts of weather, made the trip in about three weeks.

While this was a faster service than that provided by the early steamers, Californians still felt that twenty-one days was a long time to have to wait for news from their former homes to reach them. Within the next few years new stage lines were organized which, following more direct routes, cut the time to fifteen days or less.

Then, as the decade of the 1860s opened, there was launched a new mail service, one that has ever since been regarded as one of the most picturesque ventures in the history of the early West. This was, of course, the

48

famous Pony Express, by which a group of young riders, many of them still in their 'teens, mounted on swift ponies and changing to fresh mounts every few miles, dashed between Sacramento and a town on the Missouri River in ten days, and sometimes less. The express riders, bearing their letters and papers in leather pouches, carried no weapons on their swift passage across the plains and deserts, depending on the speed of their ponies to avoid attacks by the warlike Indians of the region.

Although the service it offered was much faster than that of the steamers or stagecoaches, the Pony Express continued to operate for only a little more than a year and a half. For a new and far speedier means of communication —the telegraph—was then coming into general use, and throughout most of 1861 crews were busy stringing the wires across the western third of the nation. When their task was completed on October 26 of that year, the brief reign of the Pony Express riders drew to a close.

While the Overland Telegraph, by putting Californians in instant touch with the rest of the world, did much to relieve the sense of isolation they had long felt, transportation to and from the east coast was still a slow and tedious process. Almost from the beginning of the gold rush, residents had been

49

looking forward to the day when a railroad would be built across the continent, over which they could travel in comfort, and goods could be carried speedily and at a moderate cost.

Proposals for the building of such a road had been made at intervals throughout the 1850s. It was not, however, until after the outbreak of the Civil War in 1861 that a start was made. Two companies, each of which received liberal help from the national government, were organized. One, called the Union Pacific, began laying rails westward from Council Bluffs on the Missouri River. The other, the Central Pacific, pushed eastward from Sacramento.

During the next seven years this great work was carried forward with all possible speed, and in the face of many difficulties. For not only did its route pass over hundreds of miles of uninhabited plains and deserts, but two rugged mountain ranges, the Rockies and the Sierra Nevada, had to be crossed. When at last, on May 10, 1869, the two construction crews met at Promontory Point, in the present state of Utah, and the rails were joined, the event was celebrated all over the country. The rejoicing was particularly keen among the Californians, who realized that their many years of isolation from the rest of the nation had finally come to an end.

*Chapter XI*

# THE MODERN STATE

THE driving of the last spike at Promontory Point ushered in a new and exciting era in the history of the state. The pioneer period then drew to a close, and each year thereafter saw changes in many fields. The trains of the railroad daily brought carloads of newcomers from other parts of the nation, not only tourists on brief visits but settlers who planned to make their homes there. As population grew, many of the huge ranches of earlier days were divided into smaller farms. Orchards and vineyards were set out, crops of various kinds were planted, and from one end of the state to the other scores of new villages and towns sprang up.

Only in the great central valleys was this breaking up of large holdings into small ones long delayed. There for another two decades the big wheat ranches continued to be operated. On many of them workmen numbering into the hundreds were busy each spring and fall planting and harvesting the crops. The sacked wheat was then hauled to the nearest railroad, or loaded on river barges, and carried down to San Francisco Bay. In the vicinity of the towns of Port Costa and Crockett miles of huge warehouses had been built to receive it. There it was transferred into the holds of fast sailing ships, known as the grain fleet, and carried to Europe, the Orient, and other distant points.

Meantime throughout the southern half of the state changes no less far-reaching were taking place. In increasing number settlers, attracted by the mild climate and the fertility of the soil, took over the former cattle ranges, and the once-sleepy towns of the Spanish and Mexican eras grew and prospered. During the earlier period residents of this area experimented with the growing of many different kinds of crops. Large fields of cotton

were set out and thousands of mulberry trees planted, the latter to provide food for silkworms, for it was believed the region would become a great silk-producing center.

It was not, however, until the introduction in the late 1870s of a new and superior variety of oranges that southern California growers found their ideal crop. Although oranges had been grown in the mission gardens by the Spanish priests many years earlier, the fruit was small, full of seeds, and of inferior flavor. With the planting of the new trees, bearing much larger and more tasteful fruit, the industry grew by leaps and bounds. Today southern California is one of the world's leading producers of oranges, lemons, and other citrus fruits, each season growing and packing and shipping millions of boxes.

At the same time the area's rise as a vacation land and recreation center also began, and this, too, has continued ever since. With numerous beaches along its coastline offering facilities for bathing, boating, and other water sports, and with the mountains and deserts of the interior holding forth many attractions to nature lovers, the number of tourists visiting the region has grown year by year. Moreover, the healthy climate, and in particular the mild winters, has made it a favorite spot for elderly people to retire to and spend their declining years.

But although the population of southern California grew steadily all during the final quarter of the last century, it was not until after 1900 that

53

the region began to make its greatest progress. One reason for this is that in 1910 the first motion pictures were made in the little town of Hollywood, thus founding the great industry that exists there today. Another was the discovery of numerous oil fields within the area, the development of which has added immensely to its prosperity, as have also the many airplane and other manufacturing plants that have sprung up in recent years.

In the northern part of the state changes no less striking have taken place. As gold mining declined, other large industries sprang up to take its place. One of the most important of these was lumbering, with hundreds of sawmills operating in the forests of the Sierra and the Coast Range and their products being shipped to many distant places.

Agriculture, too, became a steadily more important factor in the economy of the region. Orchards and vineyards presently covered many thousands of acres in the valleys and foothills adjacent to the coast. Farther inland, the huge wheat ranches were one by one subdivided into small farms where, with the aid of irrigation, bountiful crops of many kinds were raised. Elsewhere, in districts not suitable for farming, stock raising was extensively carried on, with great herds of cattle and sheep roaming the foothill ranges and, as summer came on, being driven high into the mountains to graze on the grassy meadows there.

Meantime the big, land-locked harbor of San Francisco had become the center of a bustling world trade. From there not only were the products of the farms and mills and factories of the region shipped to the markets on the east coast and Europe, but numerous steamers carrying goods to and from China, Japan, and other countries of the Orient passed in and out of the port.

Thus, during the little more than a century that has passed since California became a part of the United States, vast and far-reaching changes

have occurred. Today the state has a population second only to New York, and contains within its borders an infinite variety of attractions, both natural and man-made. For those in quest of recreation it offers such beauty spots as the Yosemite Valley and Lake Tahoe in the Sierra, Death Valley and other picturesque desert areas in the southeast, the stately redwood groves of the northern coast, and the many ocean beaches that lie between San Diego and Santa Barbara.

Of special interest to visitors and residents alike are the old adobe buildings put up by the Spaniards more than a century and a half ago. These are to be seen at San Diego, Los Angeles, Santa Barbara, Monterey, and many other points along the coast. No less picturesque are the quaint gold towns of the Sierra foothills, many of them but little changed since the faraway period when their sidewalks resounded to the boots of the '49ers.

Present-day Californians, young and old, look back with justifiable pride on the colorful history of their state, and they regard with confidence the opportunities and challenges of the future.

MANILLA GALLEONS

RUSSIANS 1780'S

A HISTORICAL MAP OF
# CALIFORNIA
*Legend*

▭ PORTOLÁ - 1769

▱▱▱▱ ANZA - 1774

▭▭ SMITH - 1826-28

▬ ▬ TRAILS OF THE FORTY-NINERS

⬧ — MISSIONS

WHALING 1791

PACIFIC OCEAN

THE GREAT SEAL OF THE STATE OF CALIFORNIA

EUREKA

STEAMSHIPS 1849

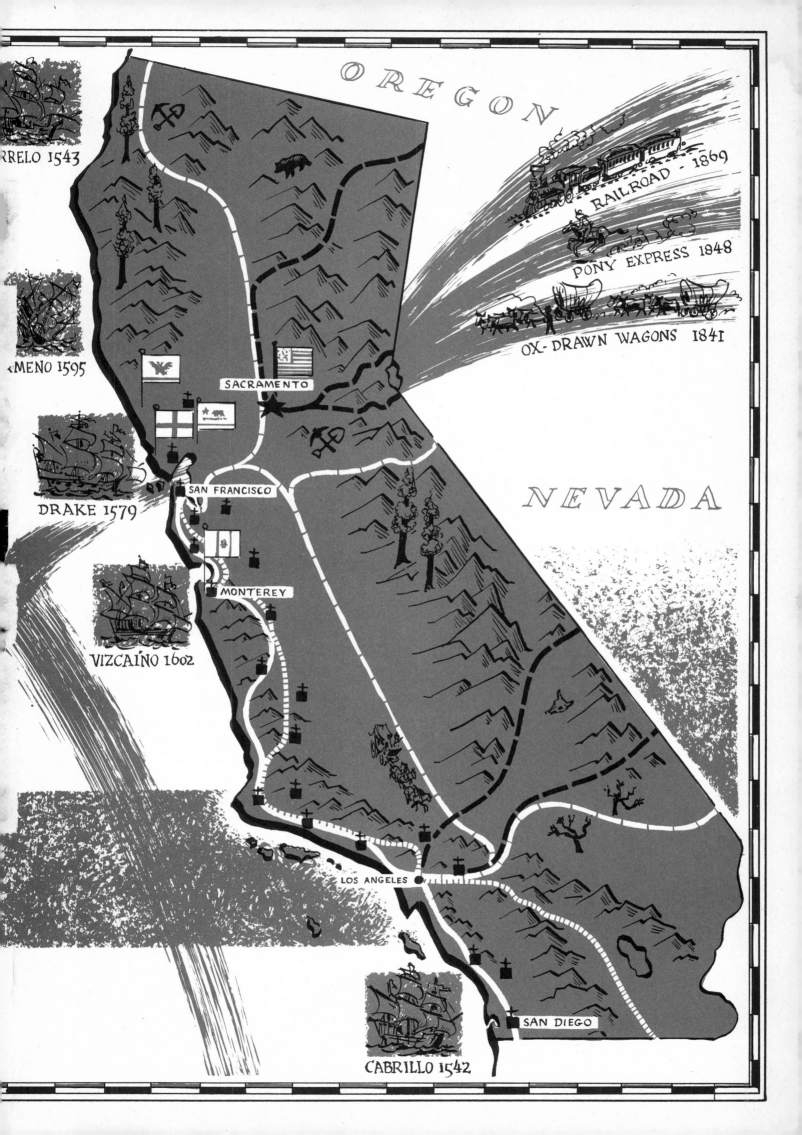

OREGON

RRELO 1543

MENO 1595

DRAKE 1579

VIZCAÍNO 1602

RAILROAD - 1869

PONY EXPRESS 1848

OX-DRAWN WAGONS 1841

NEVADA

SACRAMENTO

SAN FRANCISCO

MONTEREY

LOS ANGELES

SAN DIEGO

CABRILLO 1542